The Comprehensive Autism Planning System (CAPS) for Individuals With Autism Spectrum Disorders and Related Disabilities

Integrating Evidence-Based Practices Throughout the Student's Day

INSTRUCTOR MANUAL

Shawn A. Henry

Brenda Smith Myles, PhD

FUTURE HORIZONS

ISBN: 978-1-937473-75-4

Table of Contents

Overview of Features: Instructor Manual 1

Chapter 1. The Comprehensive Autism Planning System 3

Chapter 2. Structure/Modifications 11
            Kai-Chien Tien, PhD, and Hyo Jung Lee, PhD

Chapter 3. Reinforcement 19
            Joyce Downing, PhD

Chapter 4. Sensory Strategies 25

Chapter 5. Communication/Social Skills.....................................33
            Teresa Cardon, PhD, CCC-SLP

Chapter 6. Data Collection 41
            Andi Babkie, PhD

Chapter 7. Generalization 47

Chapter 8. Instruction Often Occurring in Specialized Settings ...51
            with Sheila M. Smith, PhD, and Sherry Moyer, MSW

Chapter 9. M-CAPS – Using CAPS in Middle School, High School,
            and Beyond..57

Chapter 10. The CAPS Process 61

References...67

Overview of Features: Instructor Manual

This instructor manual for *The Comprehensive Autism Planning System (CAPS) for Individuals With Autism Spectrum and Related Disabilities* includes the following features for instructors' use.

For Each Chapter ...

Learner Objectives – List of learner objectives as a preview of the chapter's content. The learner objectives also highlight information that readers are expected to understand and be able to explain after reading the chapter.

Chapter Summary – Overview of the main points of the chapter as a refresher prior to reviewing recommendations for in-class activities, project ideas, paper topic ideas, PowerPoint™ presentations, chapter tests, and the comprehensive exam.

Chapter Review Questions and Answers – Questions and accompanying answers designed to check understanding of and ability to explain the information discussed within the chapter. The review questions may also be used as a study guide when preparing for tests and/or exams that may be administered in class.

Glossary – Alphabetical listing of vocabulary terms presented in grey boldface within the book.

In-Class Activities – Suggestions for in-class activities related to the chapter.

Long- and Short-Term Project Ideas – Project ideas that range from those appropriate for assignment at the beginning of the semester and that are designed to be completed over the course of the semester, to those that are relevant to a specific chapter and should be assigned either prior to or following in-class discussion of a given chapter.

Paper Topic Ideas – Recommended topics for student papers.

The following instructional and support materials may be downloaded by instructors from http://www.aapcpublishing. net/9510

Chapter PowerPoint™ Presentations – Text-based PowerPoint™ presentations highlighting the main points of each chapter. Instructors may add the slide design of their choice to each presentation and modify slides as they wish. PowerPoint™ slides are reproducible for educational purposes only.

Chapter Tests – A printable test for each chapter with an accompanying answer key. Instructors may modify these as they wish. They may be shared with students as a self-check of their knowledge and understanding of a chapter's material, as a study guide, or as an in-class test or quiz. Tests are reproducible for educational purposes in your course only.

Comprehensive Exam – A comprehensive exam with an accompanying answer key that largely consists of short-answer questions intended to evaluate students' overall understanding of context blindness as presented in the book. Instructors may modify the exam as they wish. The exam may be reproduced for educational purposes in your course only.

The Comprehensive Autism Planning System

CHAPTER 1

Learner Objectives

After reading this chapter, the learner should be able to:

- State the role and purpose of the CAPS.

- List the components of the CAPS.

- Define the components of the CAPS.

- Describe the relationship between CAPS and the Ziggurat Model.

- State the five levels of the Intervention Ziggurat.

Chapter Summary

In Chapter One, Henry and Myles describe the role of the CAPS in helping professionals to know critical information "at a glance." The components of the CAPS: Time; Activity; Targeted Skills to Teach; Structure/Modification; Reinforcement; Sensory Strategies; Communication/Social Skills; Data Collection; and Generalization Plan are outlined. The Ziggurat Model, a companion model to the CAPS, is introduced. A case study illustrates implementation of the CAPS.

Glossary

Activity – this include all tasks and activities throughout the day in which the student requires support. Academic periods (e.g., reading, math), nonacademic times (e.g., recess, lunch), and transitions between classes are all examples of activities

Communication/social skills – specific communication goals or activities as well as supports are delineated here. Goals or activities may include (a) requesting help, (b) taking turns in conversation, and (c) protesting appropriately. Supports, which are also diverse, may encompass (a) language boards; (b) PECS (Picture Exchange Communication System; Frost & Bondy, 2002); and (c) other augmentative communication systems

Data collection – data collection includes gathering information on behavior(s) to be documented during a specific activity. Typically, this section relates directly to IEP goals and objectives, behavioral issues, and state standards

Generalization plan – because many individuals with ASD have problems generalizing information across settings, this section of the CAPS was developed to ensure that generalization of skills is built into the program

Intervention Ziggurat – a structure that describes the five levels of intervention that must be addressed in a comprehensive intervention

Reinforcement – student access to specific types of reinforcement as well as reinforcement schedules is listed under the reinforcement section of the CAPS

Sensory strategies – sensory supports and strategies identified by an occupational therapist are listed in this CAPS area

Structure/modifications – this can encompass a wide variety of supports, including placement in the classroom, visual supports (e.g., choice boards, visual schedules), peer supports (e.g., Circle

4

of Friends, peer buddies), and instructional strategies (e.g., priming, self-monitoring)

Targeted skills to teach – this may include IEP goals, state standards, and/or general skills that lead to school success. These skills can serve as the basis for measuring response to intervention (RTI) or annual yearly progress (AYP)

Time – this section indicates the clock time when each activity that the student engages in throughout the day takes place

Ziggurat Model – a companion model to CAPS designed to address the underlying needs of individuals with ASD using five levels of intervention

Review Questions and Answers

1. Explain how the limitations of an IEP are addressed by the CAPS.

   Answer: Even though student outcomes are delineated in the IEP, it is often difficult to fully transfer them to a student's daily program (Aspy & Grossman, 2011). Some accommodations may not be listed on the IEP even though they are integral to the student's success, leading to frustration both for the teacher and the student, limitations in access to the general education curriculum, or severe behavior challenges.

2. What is the "all-important" question answered by the CAPS?

   Answer: What supports does the student need for each activity?

3. List and describe the components of the CAPS.

   Answer:

   a. *Time.* This section indicates the clock time when each activity that the student engages in throughout the day takes place.

b. *Activity.* Activities include all tasks and activities throughout the day in which the student requires support. Academic periods (e.g., reading, math), nonacademic times (e.g., recess, lunch), and transitions between classes would all be considered activities.

c. *Targeted Skills to Teach.* This may include IEP goals, state standards, and/or general skills that lead to school success. These skills can serve as the basis for measuring response to intervention (RTI) or annual yearly progress (AYP).

d. *Structure/Modifications.* This can encompass a wide variety of supports, including placement in the classroom, visual supports (e.g., choice boards, visual schedules), peer supports (e.g., Circle of Friends, peer buddies), and instructional strategies (e.g., priming, self-monitoring).

e. *Reinforcement.* Student access to specific types of reinforcement as well as reinforcement schedules is listed under the reinforcement section of the CAPS.

f. *Sensory Strategies.* Sensory supports and strategies identified by an occupational therapist are listed in this CAPS area.

g. *Communication/Social Skills.* Specific communication goals or activities as well as supports are delineated here. Goals or activities may include (a) requesting help, (b) taking turns in conversation, and (c) protesting appropriately. Supports, which are also diverse, may encompass (a) language boards; (b) PECS (Picture Exchange Communication System; Frost & Bondy, 2002); and (c) other augmentative communication systems.

h. *Data Collection.* Data collection includes gathering information on behavior(s) to be documented during a specific activity. Typically, this section relates directly to IEP goals and objectives, behavioral issues, and state standards.

i. *Generalization Plan.* Because individuals with ASD often have problems generalizing information across settings, this section of the CAPS was developed to ensure that generalization of skills is built into the student's program.

4. Describe the components of the Ziggurat Model and its relationship to the CAPS.

   Answer: The Ziggurat Model is designed to address true needs or underlying deficits that result in social, emotional, and behavioral concerns. The Intervention Ziggurat contains five levels organized in a hierarchical structure. Starting with the foundation level – Sensory Differences and Biological Needs – each level represents an area that must be addressed in order for an intervention to be effective. To use the Ziggurat and CAPS together, the process begins with the completion of the UCC and ISSI to identify the child's autism and his strengths and skills. Then interventions are identified in each of the five Ziggurat levels, starting with Sensory Differences and Biological Needs, so that all the UCC and ISSI items are addressed. This information is then incorporated into the CAPS to ensure that the student's needs and interventions are addressed throughout the student's daily schedule with data collection and generalization built in.

In-Class Activities

1. Fill in the chart below based on the class discussion. As a class, generate strategies that address the underlying characteristics that can be plugged into CAPS.

Challenges	Possible Related Underlying Characteristic of Autism	Strategy to Put in CAPS
Dominates when working in small groups. Insists that things be done "his way."	• Difficulty with loud settings • Poor problem-solving skills • Difficulty with the rules of conversation	
Leaves the classroom.		
Keeps working on math problems when told time is up. Does not stop until he has completed all of the items on the page.		
Wanders the playground by himself. Does not play with peers.		
Does not initiate interactions with peers. Does not join group activities unless physically guided.		

Paper Topic Ideas

1. Write a short essay about a time when you were asked to work with a student with ASD and you were uncertain about exactly what needed to be done. How did you feel? How did you decide what to do? What was the outcome? How could the outcome have improved if you had been provided with the CAPS for the student?

2. Write a short essay from Ginny's (the student in the case study in Chapter One) perspective about how "your" day at school improved after the school staff began to use the CAPS.

Short-Term Project Ideas

Interview a teacher or parent of a child with ASD. Based on the interview, fill in the chart below. List challenges that the child or student is experiencing in the first column. In the second column, list possible related underlying characteristics of autism. An example of each is provided. The UCC may be a good resource for this project.

Challenges	Possible Related Underlying Characteristic of Autism
Dominates when working in small groups. Insists that things be done "his way."	▪ Difficulty with loud settings ▪ Poor problem-solving skills ▪ Difficulty with the rules of conversation

Long-Term Project Ideas

1. Begin a collection of journal articles and critiques of research related to the effectiveness of intervention strategies for students with ASD. From a peer-reviewed journal, select two articles about intervention strategies designed for individuals with ASD. Read the original journal articles. For each article, summarize the methods and results. Discuss the strengths and limitations of the study. Critique the strengths and limitations of the strategies themselves. Finally, demonstrate how that strategy would be incorporated into the CAPS by filling in the CAPS for a student (actual or fictional) using this strategy. Place entries into each area of the CAPS that applies.

2. Based on the current interventions and schedule, fill out the CAPS on a student with whom you work.

Structure/ Modifications

CHAPTER 2

Learner Objectives

After reading this chapter, the learner should be able to:

- Describe the purpose of the Structure/Modifications column of the CAPS.

- List and describe structure modification strategies that are often helpful to students with ASD.

- List and describe academic modification strategies that are often helpful to students with ASD.

- Explain the statement "CAPS is methodology-friendly."

Chapter Summary

In Chapter Two, the authors describe the purpose of the Structure/ Modifications column of the CAPS. Structure/modification, including environmental and academic supports, are essential components of the CAPS model. Structure and modifications can help students across the spectrum to show their competence.

Glossary

Boundary markers – strong visual cues that can be used throughout the classroom to guide students with ASD and their peers through physical spaces

Choice board – an alternative way of presenting choices by visually exhibiting them

Early/late release – providing the student extra time to reach a destination in a relatively stress-free environment

Graphic organizers – tools such as semantic maps, Venn diagrams, outlines, and charts used to organize content material in a visual way that makes it easier to understand

Home base – a quiet place in the school where students can go to (a) plan or review information or (b) cope with stress and behavioral challenges. It also serves as a place students can go if (a) they feel the classroom is becoming overwhelming, (b) a teacher thinks a meltdown may be on the way, or (c) they need a place to calm from overstimulation

Lists/task cards – ways of presenting information to students with ASD by giving them something to refer to. They may include information that would typically be presented only verbally, such as instructions, or information that would not be presented at all because it is assumed knowledge

Priming – a preview of activities and an overview of assignments or schedule changes

Signals and cues – subtle methods that adults use to prompt students to attend and respond

Structure/modifications – a wide variety of supports, including placement in the classroom, visual supports (e.g., choice boards, visual schedules), peer supports (e.g., Circle of Friends, peer buddies), and instructional strategies (e.g., priming, self-monitoring)

Visual schedules – visual presentation of a student's schedule that takes an abstract concept, such as time, and presents it in a more concrete and manageable form. Visual schedules allow students to anticipate upcoming events and activities, develop an understanding of time, and facilitate the ability to predict change

Review Questions and Answers

1. List and describe some of the environmental considerations that are listed in the CAPS's Structure/Modifications column.

   Answer:

   a. Classroom layout –

      i. Clearly defined areas for each activity

      ii. Visual reminders of classroom expectations

      iii. Adequate spacing to allow for personal space preferences, such as sitting at least 24" from another person

      iv. Clear and consistent organization of materials; for example, by color coding and labeling (with written words, pictures, or both)

   b. Home base – a quiet place in the school where students can go to (a) plan or review information or (b) cope with stress and behavioral challenges. It also serves as a place students can go if (a) they feel the classroom is becoming overwhelming, (b) a teacher thinks a meltdown may be on the way, or (c) students need a place to calm from overstimulation

   c. Visual schedules – visual representations of upcoming events or activities designed to meet the student's need for predictability

   d. Lists/task cards – ways of presenting information to students with ASD by giving them something to refer to. This may include information that would typically be presented only verbally, such as instructions, or information that would not be presented at all because it is assumed knowledge

e. Choice boards – an alternative way of presenting choices by visually exhibiting them

f. Boundary markers – strong visual cues that can be used throughout the classroom to guide students with ASD and their peers through physical spaces

2. List at least four alternatives to having a student write a response.

Answer:

a. Responding orally

b. Keyboarding

c. Answering questions in a true/false or multiple-choice format instead of an essay format

d. Reading answers into a tape recorder

e. Using a scribe

3. Explain the purpose of priming.

Answer: Given an opportunity to preview activities before they will occur, the student is often less likely to experience anxiety and stress about what lies ahead. With anxiety and stress at a minimum, the student can then focus his efforts on successfully completing assignments and other activities.

4. List and describe some academic modifications that may be included on CAPS.

Answer: Graphic organizers, such as semantic maps, Venn diagrams, outlines, and charts, organize content material in a visual way that makes it easier to understand. Assignments and tests may be modified by length or format to meet a student's needs. Priming may be provided to prepare the student for an activity that he will be expected to complete in the near future.

5. Explain the statement "CAPS is methodology-friendly."

Answer: CAPS has the built-in flexibility so it can be used with almost any intervention approach. CAPS can be used with any of the NAC-identified treatment models.

In-Class Activities

1. Use the list of strategies from Short-Term Project #1 as a basis for this in-class activity. Have the class members compile their results (perhaps by a simple tally) and place the data into the table below. As a class, discuss how the results would impact the services received by a student with ASD. Discuss how the CAPS may be used to identify and address areas in which staff training is needed and how CAPS may be used to create systems level changes.

	Educational Assistant		General Education Teacher		Special Education Teacher	
	Familiar	Ready to Implement	Familiar	Ready to Implement	Familiar	Ready to Implement
Boundary Markers						
Graphic Organizers						
Priming						
Choice Board						
Home Base						
Signals and Cues						
Early/Late Release						
Lists/Task Cards						
Visual Schedules						

2. Generate a list of visual supports that members of the class have used during the course of their day prior to attending class. Discuss the role of visual supports for most well-functioning adults. Discuss the characteristics of ASD that may make visual supports even more valuable for individuals with ASD

Paper Topic Ideas

1. With a student with whom you are familiar in mind, write a sample letter to the student's parent explaining how the home base strategy will be used for his or her child with ASD. Explain where the home base will be, when the student will go to home base, what the student will do there, and how this strategy is expected to benefit the student. Be sure to make clear in your letter that home base is not the same as timeout.

2. Write a short essay describing how the CAPS itself is a structure/modification strategy. Include in your essay elements that the CAPS has in common with priming, graphic organizers, visual schedules, and assignment modifications.

Short-Term Project Ideas

1. Make three copies of the following list of structure/modification strategies. Provide a separate copy of the list of strategies to an educational assistant (EA), a general education teacher, and a special education teacher, each of whom is working with a student who has ASD. Ask each to check the column that best describes his or her knowledge of the strategies listed.

Staff Position:			
	Unfamiliar	Familiar	Ready to Implement
Boundary Markers			
Graphic Organizers			
Priming			
Choice Board			
Home Base			
Signals and Cues			
Early/Late Release			
Lists/Task Cards			
Visual Schedules			

Write a brief summary of the results. Discuss how the results would impact the services received by a student with ASD. Explain how the CAPS may be used to identify and address areas in which staff training is needed.

Long-Term Project Ideas

1. Continue your collection of journal articles and critiques of research related to the effectiveness of intervention strategies for students with ASD. From a peer-reviewed journal, select two articles about Structure/Modification intervention strategies designed for individuals with ASD. Read the original journal articles. For each article, summarize the methods and results. Discuss the strengths and limitations of the study. Critique the strengths and limitations of the strategies themselves. Finally, demonstrate how the strategy would be incorporated into the CAPS by filling in the CAPS for a student (actual or fictional) using this strategy. Place entries into each area of the CAPS that applies.

2. Add at least three structure/modification strategies to the CAPS that you created for Chapter One. Highlight the new strategies on the CAPS.

Reinforcement

CHAPTER 3

Learner Objectives

After reading this chapter, the learner should be able to:

- Describe the purpose of the Reinforcement column of the CAPS.

- Explain the purpose of all reinforcement strategies.

- List three categories of reinforcers and provide examples of each.

- Explain the guidelines for delivering and troubleshooting reinforcement.

Chapter Summary

In Chapter Three, the author describes the purpose of the Reinforcement column of the CAPS. Research has unequivocally shown that reinforcement is an essential component in learning. In fact, according to Aspy and Grossman (2011), without reinforcement there is no learning. CAPS supports this concept by ensuring that reinforcement is considered throughout the student's day.

Glossary

Contingent reinforcement – reinforcement that is given if and when a specified behavior is performed

Reinforcement – delivering a specific consequence when the student demonstrates a target behavior to increase the likelihood that the behavior will occur again when requested

Review Questions and Answers

1. How are reinforcers to be included on the CAPS selected?

   Answer: As part of CAPS, reinforcers must be selected carefully, based on the student's needs and characteristics. For example, Billy may find a high-five for completing his work very reinforcing, but for Adrienne, who is preoccupied with germs and avoids casual physical contact, it would likely have an adverse effect. Strategies for selecting reinforcers include (a) observing preferences and choices in natural settings, (b) asking students what they would like to work for, and (c) interviewing parents or teachers to determine what has worked in the past.

   Another way to select reinforcers, as well as to identify replacement behaviors, is to consider the function of the student's problem behavior. Most behaviors are instrumental; that is, students engage in certain behaviors to either "get" or "get out of" something. The role of the team is to develop a hypothesis about why problem behavior occurs, based on patterns of classroom behavior. The hypothesis can be used to select replacement behaviors and reinforcers that address the function – or purpose – of the behavior in more acceptable ways.

2. What are the guidelines for delivering reinforcement?

   Answer: The reinforcement must be contingent on the target behavior; that is, the student only earns the predetermined consequence if and when she performs the requested behavior. Another important consideration is the schedule of reinforcement used. When teaching a new behavior to mastery, or introducing a replacement behavior to address a problem, reinforcement is generally delivered on a one-to-one (1:1) basis. That means that for every instance of the target behavior, the student receives the reinforcer. After the student has demonstrated fluency in the new skill, the ratio of behaviors to reinforcer can be raised gradually.

3. What questions should a team ask when troubleshooting the effectiveness of reinforcement in a student's plan?

   Answer:

   - Were the task requirements and the selected consequence clearly stated by the adult and understood by the student?

   - Was the target behavior a task the student could perform without prompting?

   - Was the reinforcer chosen by the student and sufficiently desirable?

   - Was the reinforcer delivered immediately following the target behavior?

   - If the desired behavior replaced a previous problem behavior, did the replacement behavior and reinforcer address the function of the student's original behavior?

In-Class Activities

1. Generate a list of reinforcers that members of the class have used during the course of their day prior to attending class. Discuss the role of reinforcers for most well-functioning adults. Discuss the importance of carefully selecting reinforcers that are meaningful to the individual. Why is this especially important for individuals with ASD?

2. Divide students into small groups and instruct them to discuss what role reinforcement plays in their own lives (e.g., paychecks; first do laundry, then watch favorite television show). Ask them to select two examples to share with the class when you regroup. As a class, share these examples and discuss strategies for helping team members who may be reluctant to use reinforcement better understand its potential benefits and its role in day-to-day activities.

3. Utilize the troubleshooting questions as a class to review the reinforcers being used in the ongoing case studies. Generate a list of alternative reinforcers to add to the student's menu.

   - Were the task requirements and the selected consequence clearly stated by the adult and understood by the student?

   - Was the target behavior a task the student could perform without prompting?

   - Was the reinforcer chosen by the student and sufficiently desirable?

   - Was the reinforcer delivered immediately following the target behavior?

   - If the desired behavior replaced a previous problem behavior, did the replacement behavior and reinforcer address the function of the student's original behavior?

4. Create three charts entitled Social/Activity, Tangible/Edible, and Generalized/Token. Divide the class into three groups. Have each group begin at one of the three charts. Give the groups 3-5 minutes to generate a list of potential reinforcers in the category on the chart. Reinforce the group that generates the most items. After the 3-to-5-minute time period, have the groups rotate to the next chart and add as many new reinforcers as they can generate for that chart category. Rotate for a third time. Discuss the compiled lists. Discuss how the reinforcement for generating the most items influenced the activity. Provide a copy of the compiled list to each class member.

Paper Topic Ideas

Write a brief essay about the importance of reinforcement for students with ASD. What is the purpose of reinforcement? How would the educational progress of students with ASD be impacted if all reinforcements were removed from the school day?

Short-Term Project Ideas

1. Interview a special education teacher, a general education teacher, and an educational assistant who all work with the same student who has ASD. Ask the following questions.

   a. How would you define reinforcement?

   b. What reinforcers do you use with your students who have ASD?

   c. How do you decide when to give a reinforcer?

   d. Is it ever fair to have different students in the same classroom on different reinforcement systems? If so, when?

      Write a summary of the responses. Address the following questions: From the perspective of the student who has ASD, is reinforcement frequent enough? Is it clear to you, the student, how you will earn a reinforcer? Is your school staff doing a good job of helping you by reinforcing skills that are challenging for you?

2. Write an outline of a staff or parent training entitled Reinforcement for Students With ASD.

Long-Term Project Ideas

1. Continue your collection of journal articles and critiques of research related to the effectiveness of intervention strategies for students with ASD. From a peer-reviewed journal, select two articles about reinforcement strategies designed for individuals with ASD. Read the original journal articles. For each article, summarize the methods and results. Discuss the strengths and limitations of the study. Critique the strengths and limitations of the strategies themselves. Finally, demonstrate how the strategy would be incorporated into the CAPS by filling in the CAPS for a student (actual or fictional) using this strategy. Place entries into each area of the CAPS that applies.

2. Add at least three reinforcement strategies to the CAPS that you created for Chapter One. Highlight the new strategies on the CAPS.

Sensory Strategies

CHAPTER 4

Learner Objectives

After reading this chapter, the learner should be able to:

- Describe the current status of research on sensory-based strategies for individuals with ASD.

- List and describe the seven individual sensory systems.

- List and describe the five steps of the sensory integration process.

- Explain the discriminative and protective functions of sensory experiences.

- List possible signs of ineffective sensory processing.

- Describe the role of the occupational therapist in designing sensory supports.

Chapter Summary

In Chapter Four, the author describes the purpose of the Sensory Strategies column of the CAPS. It is well documented that many individuals with ASD have significant sensory challenges. To prepare these students to learn and to support them while learning, sensory strategies can be an essential component in planning an effective daily schedule. The CAPS recognizes that for students who require sensory supports, such supports may be needed throughout the day. An occupational therapist (OT) trained in sensory integration, an essential member of the CAPS team, is a must when designing and implementing sensory supports.

Glossary

Auditory – provides information about sounds in the environment (loud, soft, high, low, near, far)

Execution – the final step of sensory processing, which involves responding or not reacting to a sensation

Gustatory – provides information about different types of taste (sweet, sour, bitter, salty, spicy)

Interpretation – linking present sensory experience to past experience

Modulation – the ability to balance or regulate the sensory systems

Olfactory – provides information about different types of smell (musty, acrid, putrid, flowery, pungent)

Organization – the stage of sensory processing when the brain decides what to do in response to the sensation

Orientation – the stage of sensory processing when the input is attended to

Proprioception – provides information about where a certain body part is and how it is moving

Registration – becoming aware of a sensation

Tactile – provides information about the environment and qualities of objects (touch, pressure, texture, hard, soft, sharp, dull, heat, cold, pain)

Vestibular – provides information about where our body is in space and whether or not we or our surroundings are moving. Tells about the speed and direction of movement

Visual – provides information about objects and persons. Helps us to define boundaries as we move through time and space

Review Questions and Answers

1. What is the current status of research on sensory-based strategies for individuals with ASD?

   Answer: While not considered by some (cf. National Research Council, 2001) as an evidence-based practice, the argument can be made that sensory-based strategies can at least be identified as promising.

2. What are the seven sensory systems? List and describe each.

   Answer:

   a. Tactile – provides information about the environment and qualities of objects (touch, pressure, texture, hard, soft, sharp, dull, heat, cold, pain)

   b. Vestibular – provides information about where our body is in space and whether or not we or our surroundings are moving. Tells about speed and direction of movement

   c. Proprioception – provides information about where a certain body part is and how it is moving

   d. Visual – provides information about objects and persons. Helps us define boundaries as we move through time and space

   e. Auditory – provides information about sounds in the environment (loud, soft, high, low, near, far)

   f. Gustatory – provides information about different types of taste (sweet, sour, bitter, salty, spicy)

   g. Olfactory – provides information about different types of smell (musty, acrid, putrid, flowery, pungent)

3. What are the steps of sensory integration?

   Answer:

   a. First, we register or become aware of the sensation.

   b. Then we orient or pay attention to it.

27

c. Next, we attempt to interpret the sensation by using current information and referencing past experiences for comparison.

d. Organization occurs when our brain decides what we should do in response to the sensation.

e. The final step is execution, or what we actually do.

4. Describe the discriminative and protective functions of the sensory experience.

   Answer: Each system has a *discriminative component* that supplies details for the central nervous system to consider. For example, when a person touches (tactile) an object, the tactile system provides information about where the touch is occurring (on the hand, not on the head) as well as whether the object is hard, soft, fuzzy, smooth, round, angular, etc. Accurate information about these attributes helps us interpret the object so that we can respond appropriately. The sensory systems also have a *protective function* that helps to protect us from harm. For example, when we reach into a shoe and detect something soft and fuzzy, the tactile system may signal us to move our hand quickly to keep from being bitten by a spider.

5. Explain how sensory processing challenges may affect learning.

   Answer: Children with sensory processing challenges are often not available to learn. They are bothered by seemingly minor stimuli that others ignore; they cannot concentrate; and once upset, they cannot inherently self-calm. Ineffective sensory processing can be a strong factor in a child's academic or social failure.

6. What are the keys to providing sensory interventions for students with ASD?

   Answer: It is important that an OT trained in sensory integration design intervention. Sensory supports must match the child's need and be embedded in the student's schedule.

In-Class Activities

1. Generate a list of sensory strategies that class members often use during this class (wiggle feet, chew gum, wear a sweater, sit near the speaker, etc). Discuss how these strategies help them to modulate their sensory systems and to improve their academic functioning. Discuss how the sensory needs of the class members compare to those of students with ASD.

2. Divide students into small groups. Provide each group with the following table. Instruct the groups to complete the table. Follow up with a large-group discussion and comparison of ideas generated by the small groups.

Evidence of Ineffective Sensory Processing	Sensory System or Systems Involved	Possible Sensory Intervention (after OT consult)
Cannot tolerate tags on shirts		
Startles easily and does not readily calm afterward		
Avoids playground equipment		
Covers ears or screams when encountering sudden loud noises, such as coming from a vacuum cleaner or the toilet flushing		
Reacts strongly when someone brushes against her in line		
Cannot tolerate the smell of fabric softener on a peer's shirt		
Looks at the teacher when she talks but has difficulty screening out irrelevant stimuli, such as the buzz of the fluorescent lights		
Has difficulty with activities that involve motor planning, such as participating in sports, carrying a lunch tray, opening a milk carton, tying shoes, or riding a bicycle		
Has difficulty writing with a pencil or pen because he cannot tell how much pressure to apply to hold the writing implement or experiences discomfort when gripping it		

3. Invite an occupational therapist who works with children with ASD and addresses sensory needs as a guest speaker in your class. Ask the OT to address the following:

   a. What sensory differences do students with ASD experience?

   b. How do you help to address those differences?

   c. What do you wish more teachers knew about sensory needs and ASD?

Paper Topic Ideas

1. Write a brief essay about how you use sensory strategies in order to get through a typical day. What would happen if you were unable to modulate sensory input?

2. Write a brief description of a student with whom you have worked who has a sensory diet. What are the sensory differences that the student has? What sensory strategies are used? How do the sensory strategies help the student?

Short-Term Project Ideas

1. Interview an occupational therapist who works with children with ASD. Complete the following table based on the interview.

Evidence of Ineffective Sensory Processing	Sensory System or Systems Involved	Possible Sensory Intervention (after OT consult)
Cannot tolerate tags on shirts		
Startles easily and does not readily calm afterward		
Avoids playground equipment		
Covers ears or screams when encountering sudden loud noises, such as coming from a vacuum cleaner or the toilet flushing		
Reacts strongly when someone brushes against her in line		
Cannot tolerate the smell of fabric softener on a peer's shirt		
Looks at the teacher when she talks but has difficulty screening out irrelevant stimuli, such as the buzz of the fluorescent lights		
Has difficulty with activities that involve motor planning, such as participating in sports, carrying a lunch tray, opening a milk carton, tying shoes, or riding a bicycle		
Has difficulty writing with a pencil or pen because he cannot tell how much pressure to apply to hold the writing implement or experiences discomfort when gripping it		

2. Interview an occupational therapist who works in the public schools. Write a brief summary of his or her answers to the following questions:

   a. What sensory differences do students with ASD experience?

   b. How do you help to address those differences?

   c. What do you wish more teachers knew about sensory needs and ASD?

Long-Term Project Ideas

1. Continue your collection of journal articles and critiques of research related to the effectiveness of intervention strategies for students with ASD. From a peer-reviewed journal, select two articles about sensory interventions designed for individuals with ASD. Read the original journal articles. For each article, summarize the methods and results. Discuss the strengths and limitations of the study. Critique the strengths and limitations of the strategies themselves. Finally, demonstrate how the strategy would be incorporated into the CAPS by filling in the CAPS for a student (actual or fictional) using this strategy. Place entries into each area of the CAPS that applies.

2. Add at least three sensory strategies to the CAPS that you created for Chapter One. Highlight the new strategies on the CAPS.

Communication/ Social Skills

CHAPTER 5

Learner Objectives

After reading this chapter, the learner should be able to:

- Describe the role of motivation in initiation.

- Explain the importance of initiations and describe the three categories of initiations.

- Explain the importance of self-awareness and describe several instructional strategies that have been created specifically to target self-awareness in individuals with ASD.

- Describe strategies for teaching individuals with ASD to initiate.

- List and describe strategies for teaching individuals with ASD to communicate.

Chapter Summary

In Chapter Five, the author describes the purpose of the Communication and Social Skills column of the CAPS. The chapter focuses on struggles that individuals with ASD experience with communication and social skills. The author introduces a variety of strategies for use in individual and group instruction that may be beneficial to individuals with ASD and, therefore, need to be considered when completing the CAPS for a student.

Glossary

Assistive technology – any item, piece of equipment, or product system, whether acquired commercially off the shelf, modified, or customized, that is used to increase, maintain, or improve functional capabilities of individuals with disabilities

Conversation starters – a social strategy that utilizes small cards listing several topics that would be considered "current" and appropriate conversation topics for a particular peer group

Echolalia – repeated speech that has little or no meaning

Expressive communication – the communication of ideas, desires, or intentions

The Incredible 5-Point Scale – a self-awareness tool; the individual with ASD describes each of five points on a scale in his or her own words and the actions that need to be taken at each point

Initiations – independently created communicative acts

Natural aided language system – a classroom-based augmentative communication intervention that pairs spoken verbal language with visual supports in a variety of natural contexts throughout the day

Picture Exchange Communication System – an alternative form of communication based on the principles of applied behavior analysis that teaches individuals to use pictures to express themselves

Pivotal response training – an empirically based intervention that includes using motivational procedures and natural reinforcers in natural environments. Critical features of PRT include intensity and consistency of the intervention, family involvement, a functional approach to problem behaviors, and motivation

Power Cards – scripts of social scenarios that incorporate an individual's special interest as a motivating factor to increase his or her understanding of the social situations

Pragmatics – the set of social rules that govern the conversational use of language

Receptive communication – understanding, or comprehending, communication

Self-awareness – ability to understand one's own feelings and behaviors

Self-calming routines – relaxation techniques that may be implemented when anxiety may be heightened; plans for self-calming are discussed before a state of dysregulation is reached

Sign language – a communication system that involves the use of body movements to communicate

Social script – a strategy to help a person with ASD by providing direct language to use in a particular social scenario

Social Stories™ – a narrative of a social encounter that breaks the encounter into manageable parts that can be explained and sorted in detail; Social Stories provide a unique opportunity to look at the different perspectives people may take when experiencing the same situation

Special interests – areas of interest that may be utilized to increase the desire to interact and socialize; these interests may form the basis for creating structured opportunities to practice social skills

Stress thermometer – a visual tool that can support individuals in identifying their bodies' "stress signals;" the thermometer also lists relaxation techniques and suggestions, making specific strategies readlly available

Review Questions and Answers

1. What is the role of motivation in initiation?

   Answer: Research suggests that children with autism initiate more for items or activities that are motivating (Koegel & Koegel, 2006).

2. Explain the importance of initiations and describe the three categories of initiations.

   Answer: Initiating is more challenging than responding because children have to create their own independent thoughts and ideas and are not able to get ideas from or build on someone else's questions or comments. A child who can initiate will be able to get others to respond to him, and in turn improve his overall communication and language skills. Initiations are broken down into three categories: behavior regulation, social communication, and joint attention. When children initiate for behavior regulation, it is to get their basic needs met – requests for food, drink, comfort, etc. Initiations for social communication are about two people interacting. At this level, children initiate to ask questions, take turns, gain information, and relate with another person. Finally, at the joint attention level, children initiate to simultaneously attend with another person to an event or an object. In other words, they initiate to share a single focus.

3. What strategies are used to teach individuals with ASD to initiate?

   Answer: The Picture Exchange Communication System, sign language, pivotal response training, assistive technology, and the natural aided language system.

4. Explain the relationship between self-awareness and self-calming.

   Answer: Persons with ASD demonstrate varying degrees of ability to understand their own feelings. As a result, many do not detect how they feel and hence do not know when to self-calm, for example. This is compounded by the challenges of many individuals with ASD when trying to understand what self-calming strategies are available and how to use them.

5. List and describe strategies for teaching individuals with ASD to communicate that may be included on the CAPS.

   Answer:

   Picture Exchange Communication System – an alternative form of communication based on the principles of applied behavior analysis that teaches individuals to use pictures to express themselves

   Sign language – a communication system that involves the use of body movements to communicate

   Pivotal Response Training – an empirically based intervention that includes using motivational procedures and natural reinforcers in natural environments. Critical features of PRT include intensity and consistency of the intervention, family involvement, a functional approach to problem behaviors, and motivation

   Assistive technology – any item, piece of equipment, or product system, whether acquired commercially off the shelf, modified, or customized, that is used to increase, maintain, or improve functional capabilities of individuals with disabilities

   Natural aided language system – a classroom-based augmentative communication intervention that pairs spoken verbal language with visual supports in a variety of natural contexts throughout the day

6. List and describe some social skills interventions that may be included on the CAPS

   Answer:

   Social Stories™ – a narrative of a social encounter that breaks the encounter into manageable parts that can be explained and sorted in detail; Social Stories provide a unique opportunity to look at the different perspectives people may take when experiencing the same situation

   Social script – a strategy to help a person with ASD by providing direct language to use in a particular social scenario

Power Cards – scripts of social scenarios that incorporate an individual's special interest as a motivating factor to increase his or her understanding of the social situations

Conversation starters – a social strategy that utilizes small cards listing several topics that would be considered "current" and appropriate conversation topics for a particular peer group

Special interests – areas of interest that may be utilized to increase the desire to interact and socialize; these interests may form the basis for creating structured opportunities to practice social skills

In-Class Activities

1. Divide the class into small groups. Have the groups develop conversation starters for students to use with their peers. Vary the age and situation for each group. Possible variations include: 8-year-olds at lunch at school on Monday; 16-year-olds entering art class; 6-year-olds at recess the day before Halloween; 19-year-old job applicants in a waiting room with other applicants; 15-year-olds at a school dance. Share the conversation starters as a large group. Discuss how the group culture affects what topics are appropriate. As a group, place the strategy into the CAPS for each case. Consider each area of the CAPS that would be impacted by this strategy.

2. Have members of the class share the special interest of individuals with ASD with whom they are working. Generate a list of activities that could be planned around each interest to help to structure opportunities for social interaction. Encourage creativity as well as practicality. As a group, place the strategy into the CAPS for each individual. Consider each area of the CAPS that would be impacted by this strategy.

Paper Topic Ideas

1. Write a brief essay about a high-anxiety situation that you sometimes face. What self-calming strategies do you use to cope with it? What would happen in that situation if you could not tell how you were feeling until you were overwhelmed by anxiety?

2. Write a brief description of a student with ASD who has no verbal communication with whom you have worked. How does the student communicate in order to seek attention? Ask for help? Show affection? Express anxiety?

   What level of initiation has the student mastered: Behavior regulation? Social communication? Joint attention? Explain.

Short-Term Project Ideas

1. Develop a Power Card to help an individual with ASD with whom you are familiar. Provide the card to the individual and help him or her to practice the steps. Write a brief summary of the individual's response to the Power Card.

2. Develop a self-calming routine for a student with whom you work. Create a visual support for the routine. Complete a CAPS for the student that includes the self-calming routine and use of the visual support in the daily schedule.

Long-Term Project Ideas

1. Continue your collection of journal articles and critiques of research related to the effectiveness of intervention strategies for students with ASD. From a peer-reviewed journal, select two articles about communication and social skill interventions designed for individuals with ASD. Read the original journal articles. For each article, summarize the methods and results. Discuss the strengths and limitations of the study. Critique the strengths and limitations of the strategies themselves. Finally, demonstrate how the strategy would be incorporated into the CAPS by filling in the CAPS for a student (actual or fictional) using this strategy. Place entries into each area of the CAPS that applies.

2. Add at least three communication or social skill strategies to the CAPS that you created for Chapter One. Highlight the new strategies on the CAPS.

Data Collection

Learner Objectives

After reading this chapter, the learner should be able to:

- List and describe the steps of the data collection process.

- Describe the different types of data collection methods and when each is best used.

- Describe important factors in determining when and where to collect data, who will collect data, and how to share and use the data that are collected.

Chapter Summary

In Chapter Six, the author describes the purpose of the Data Collection Skills column of the CAPS. The chapter focuses on collecting data on student behaviors. As part of the CAPS systematic approach to intervention, data collection allows the student and the team to measure student success in a routine and systematic fashion.

Glossary

Data collection – gathering information about how an individual is performing in terms of a specific social or academic behavior

Duration recording – an exact measure of behavior; a measure of how long a behavior persists

Event recording – an exact measure of behavior, a count/tally of how many times behavior occurs, used for discrete behaviors (those that have a definite beginning and end)

Latency recording – an exact measure of behavior; a measure of how long it takes to begin something

Target behaviors – more discrete behaviors, representing a step on the way toward achieving the objective

Time sampling – an estimate of behaviors; used for ongoing or high-frequency behaviors; a record of whether a behavior is or is not occurring at the end of every specific period of time

Review Questions and Answers

1. What is the purpose of collecting data as part of the CAPs process?

   Answer: Data are collected to determine both the efficacy of the intervention and the appropriateness of the goals and objectives.

2. Explain the six steps of the data collection process.

   Answer:

   a. Establishing the target behavior – Target behaviors are generally more discrete behaviors, representing a step on the way toward achieving the objective. Once the target behavior is selected, it is important to make sure it is described in terms that are specific, objective, and measurable.

b. Deciding on a system for collecting the data – This step involves selecting a system for data collection that matches the behavior.

c. Determining when and where data will be collected – This decision takes into account the potential influence on the behavior of different environments, different classes/subjects, different groups, different activities, and different teachers. In addition, to maximize the picture of the behavior and the quality of the data obtained, it may be necessary to collect data at different points in time during the day and week.

d. Determining who will collect the data – Due to the comprehensive nature of CAPS, anyone working with the student could collect data on various target behaviors as appropriate. Generalization across people, activities, settings, and times remains essential for student mastery of a behavior. Additionally, for the student to assume control of his or her behavior, self-monitoring may be included as an appropriate choice.

e. Determining a system for sharing data – A visual representation makes it clear what is happening with the behavior. A general rule of thumb is to collect data and chart them until a pattern emerges.

f. Using information collected for decision-making – Based on an analysis of the data, a plan is developed for future action.

3. What types of systems are available for collecting data?

Answer:

Duration recording – an exact measure of behavior; a measure of how long a behavior persists

Event recording – an exact measure of behavior, a count/tally of how many times behavior occurs, used for discrete behaviors (those that have a definite beginning and end)

Latency recording – an exact measure of behavior; a measure of how long it takes to begin something

Time sampling – an estimate of behaviors; used for ongoing or high-frequency behaviors; a record of whether a behavior is or is not occurring at the end of every specific period of time

In-Class Activities

1. Divide the class into small groups. Have each group design a data collection strategy for the following objective in Ginny's (from Chapter One) IEP.

   Ginny will respond to greetings by peers and familiar adults via nonverbal or verbal means in 8/10 opportunities with minimum to no cueing.

   Have each group address each of the six steps of the data collection process. Then have each group share their data collection system developed for the target behavior with the whole class.

2. Guide the class through the six steps of the data collection process for the following objective found in Ginny's (from Chapter One) IEP.

   Ginny will identify whose turn it is when reviewing video, reading picture books, and watching others play with maximum assistance across a variety of stimuli with 90% success.

Paper Topic Ideas

1. Write a brief essay from the point of view of the parent of a student with ASD, explaining why it is important to you to know that school staff members are diligent and competent in collecting data on your child's progress.

2. Write a brief essay describing how data collection could help you to meet a personal goal. Include a description of the data collection system that would be most helpful to you.

Short-Term Project Ideas

1. Develop a data collection system designed to assist you in reaching a personal goal. Describe each of the six steps of the process.

2. Develop a new data collection system for an objective found in the IEP of a student with whom you work. Describe each of the six steps of the process.

Long-Term Project Ideas

1. Continue your collection of journal articles and critiques of research related to the effectiveness of intervention strategies for students with ASD. From a peer-reviewed journal, select two articles that summarize research in the area of ASD that utilizes one of the data collection processes discussed in the chapter (event recording, latency recording, duration recording, or time sampling). Read the original journal articles. For each article, summarize the methods and results. Discuss the strengths and limitations of the study. Critique the strengths and limitations of the strategies themselves. Finally, demonstrate how the data collection systems would be incorporated into the CAPS by filling in the CAPS for a student (actual or fictional) using this data collection system. Place entries into each area of the CAPS that applies.

2. Add at least three data collection strategies to the CAPS that you created for Chapter One. Highlight the new strategies on the CAPS.

Generalization

Learner Objectives

After reading this chapter, the learner should be able to:

- Describe the purpose of the Generalization column of the CAPS.

- Distinguish between generalization of skills and generalization of supports.

Chapter Summary

In Chapter Seven, the author describes the purpose of the Generalization column of the CAPS. The chapter focuses on helping students with ASD to generalize skills learned in one environment or with one person to other environments and persons. The Generalization column on the CAPS ensures that generalization is built into every phase of the student's program.

Glossary

Generalization – the ability to display a behavior/skill across people and environments

Generalization of skills – using newly acquired skills across settings, people, and events

Generalization of supports – using supports across settings

Review Questions and Answers

1. Describe the difficulties with generalization that individuals with ASD often experience?

   Answer: A significant characteristic of students with ASD is difficulty generalizing skills and behaviors learned. For example, they learn a skill in one environment and only use the skill in that setting. Or they use a particular strategy only in the presence of the adult who taught them.

2. What is the difference between generalization of supports and generalization of skills?

   Answer: Generalization of supports involves using supports across settings. Generalization of skills involves systematic programming to ensure that a child or youth generalizes newly acquired skills across settings, people, and events.

In-Class Activities

1. Have the group share a skill that a student with ASD is learning in one setting. Brainstorm as a group other settings where each skill can be exhibited. Complete the following table.

Skill	Is Used During	Can Also Be Used ...

2. Discuss strategies that encourage generalization of skills for students with ASD.

Paper Topic Ideas

1. Write a brief essay about how your life would change if you could not generalize skills from setting to setting, person to person, event to event.

2. Write a brief essay from the perspective of a parent of a student with ASD about the frustration of hearing school staff members report that your child exhibits a skill at school that you have never seen in the home setting. Describe the experience of seeing your child exhibit skills in the home setting that the school staff tells you are never exhibited at school. Do you trust what you are told?

Short-Term Project Ideas

1. Complete the following table for a student with ASD with whom you are familiar. In the first column, list a new skill that the student is exhibiting. In the second column, write the setting or situation in which the new skill is exhibited. In the third column, list possible situations to which the skills may be generalized. In the final column, describe a strategy that would encourage generalization to the new setting or situation.

Skill	Is Used During	Can Also Be Used ...	Strategy for Generalization

Long-Term Project Ideas

1. Identify a skill that a student with whom you are working has mastered in one setting or with one individual and that the student needs to generalize to another setting or person (e.g., initiating interactions, taking turns, using a schedule, self-calming). Continue your collection of journal articles and critiques of research related to the effectiveness of intervention strategies for students with ASD. From a peer-reviewed journal, select two articles about strategies for teaching the identified skill to individuals with ASD. Read the original journal articles. For each article, summarize the methods and results. Discuss the strengths and limitations of the study. Critique the strengths and limitations of the strategies themselves. Finally, demonstrate how the strategy would be incorporated into the CAPS by filling in the CAPS for a student (actual or fictional) using this strategy. Place entries into each area of the CAPS that applies.

2. Add at least three generalization strategies to the CAPS that you created for Chapter One. Highlight the new strategies on the CAPS.

Instruction Often Occurring in Specialized Settings

Learner Objectives

After reading this chapter, the learner should be able to:

- List and describe strategies for students with ASD that are often implemented outside of the general education system.

- Describe the purpose and use of the CAPS Support Development forms.

- Explain how instruction in individual or small-group settings may help a student with ASD to be more successful in the general education setting.

Chapter Summary

In Chapter Eight, the author describes strategies that are often implemented in specialized settings as well as individualized materials that facilitate the success of students with ASD. Both extensive instruction and specialized supports are needed as a part of the CAPS process. A plan must be designed to ensure that they are in place.

Glossary

Attribution retraining – a cognitive strategy for teaching students to accurately assess motivations, thoughts, words, and deeds

Cartooning – the use of visual symbols, including cartoon figures, to enhance social understanding and problem solving

Circle of Friends – a strategy designed to promote social relationships and friendships among children with and without disabilities

Emotion recognition instruction – training designed to help individuals to identify emotional and mental states

Integrated play groups – a strategy for fostering positive peer relationships by engaging individuals with ASD with "expert" peer players in a play group in a natural setting facilitated by a trained play guide

SOCCSS – a strategy to help students with social disabilities, including those with ASD, understand social situations and develop problem-solving skills by putting behavioral and social issues into a sequential format: situation, options, consequences, choices, strategies, and simulation

SODA – a social behavioral learning strategy used to help children and youth with ASD to focus on the relevant social information, process that information, and select an appropriate response – stop, observe, deliberate, act

Social autopsies – an innovative strategy developed by Lavoie (cited in Bieber, 1994) to help students with social problems to understand social mistakes, a vehicle for analyzing a social skills problem

Video-based instruction – providing new information to students with ASD in a video format

Video modeling – learning by observing and imitating behaviors in a dynamic format; used to teach new skills and to reduce anxiety

Review Questions and Answers

1. Describe the general characteristics of strategies that often occur in specialized settings.

   Answer: Strategies that often occur in specialized settings require that initial work or perhaps actual instruction take place outside the general education setting. Many of these strategies are time consuming to implement but yield results that can ultimately improve the student's skills and independent functioning in multiple environments.

2. List and briefly describe instruction strategies that often occur in specialized settings that were presented in the chapter.

   Answer:

   Circle of Friends – a strategy designed to promote social relationships and friendships among children with and without disabilities

   Emotion recognition instruction – training designed to help individuals to identify emotional and mental states

   Integrated play groups – a strategy for fostering positive peer relationships by engaging individuals with ASD with "expert" peer players in a play group in a natural setting facilitated by a trained play guide

   SOCCSS – a strategy to help students with social disabilities, including those with ASD, understand social situations and develop problem-solving skills by putting behavioral and social issues into a sequential format: situation, options, consequences, choices, strategies, and simulation

   SODA – a social behavioral learning strategy used to help children and youth with ASD to focus on the relevant social information, process that information, and select an appropriate response – stop, observe, deliberate, act

   Social autopsies – an innovative strategy developed by Lavoie (cited in Bieber, 1994) to help students with social problems to understand social mistakes; a vehicle for analyzing a social skills problem

Video-based instruction – providing new information to students with ASD in a video format

Video modeling – learning by observing and imitating behaviors in a dynamic format; used to teach new skills and to reduce anxiety

Attribution retraining – a cognitive strategy for teaching students to accurately assess motivations, thoughts, words, and deeds

Cartooning – the use of visual symbols, including cartoon figures, to enhance social understanding and problem solving

3. What is the CAPS Support Development form?

   Answer: A form used when completing the CAPS to designate what supports need to be developed and/or selected, who will develop them, who will teach use of the support, and how and when its effectiveness will be evaluated.

In-Class Activities

1. Discuss the concept of "instruction often occurring in specialized settings." Where do schools usually draw the line between general education strategies and strategies for specialized settings? Where should the line be drawn? Can some of the strategies included in this chapter be used successfully in the general education setting?

2. Present cartoons that you have used with students. Explain the situation that was being explored in the cartoon. Compare the process of cartooning with talking about a situation or telling a student exactly what to do the next time she faces a similar situation.

Paper Topic Ideas

1. Write a brief essay about why cartooning and video modeling are often more effective strategies for individuals with ASD than talking about a situation or telling a student exactly what to do the next time she faces a similar situation.

2. Write an essay about the concept of "instruction often occurring in specialized settings." Where do schools usually draw the line between general education strategies and strategies for specialized settings? Where do you think the line should be drawn? Why?

Short-Term Project Ideas

1. Complete the SOCCSS worksheet based on a social problem that you have experienced recently.

2. Complete the Social Autopsies worksheet based on a social problem that you have experienced recently.

3. Create a cartoon based on a social problem that you have experienced recently.

Short-Term Project Ideas

1. Continue your collection of journal articles and critiques of research related to the effectiveness of intervention strategies for students with ASD. From a peer-reviewed journal, select two articles about one or more of the specialized interventions discussed in Chapter Eight. Read the original journal articles. For each article, summarize the methods and results. Discuss the strengths and limitations of the study. Critique the strengths and limitations of the strategies themselves. Finally, demonstrate how the strategy would be incorporated into the CAPS by filling in the CAPS for a student (actual or fictional) using this strategy. Place entries into each area of the CAPS that applies.

2. Complete a CAPS Support Development form for the CAPS that you began for Chapter One.

M-CAPS –
Using CAPS
in Middle School,
High School,
and Beyond

Learner Objectives

After reading this chapter, the learner should be able to:

- Describe the purpose of the M-CAPS.

- List the benefits of using the M-CAPS.

- Describe uses of the M-CAPS beyond the high school years.

Chapter Summary

In Chapter Nine, the author overviews how CAPS can be used in middle and high school but with some modifications. The Modified Comprehensive Autism Planning system (M-CAPS) differs somewhat in structure from the form used during the elementary years. The M-CAPS easily communicates what the student needs to be successful across activities.

Glossary

M-CAPS – an effective means of communicating to educators what the student needs to be successful across activities

Review Questions and Answers

1. What is the M-CAPS?

   Answer: The M-CAPS is a version of the CAPS that is modified from the form used during elementary school. Some classes in middle and high school mirror in structure those that are taught in elementary school. For these classes, the traditional CAPS may be used. In other classes, students are likely to be required to participate in a mixture of (a) independent work, (b) group work, (c) tests, (d) lectures, and (e) homework. From this standpoint, the activities in English class and geometry are the same. The M-CAPS is an effective means of communicating to educators who teach academic subjects the types of supports students need during each activity in academic classes with similar formats.

2. Describe the benefits of using the M-CAPS.

   Answer: The student uses the same types of supports across classes, which allows her to see the flexibility of supports, which in turn facilitates her understanding of the concept of generalization.

   Communication is fostered across academic teachers because teachers share the same documents and have access to the same types of supports for a given student.

   The student's case manager and team can easily track successes and problems across academic subjects.

3. Describe how the M-CAPS may be utilized after high school completion.

Answer: Students with ASD who enter a two- or four-year college or university may find that the M-CAPS provides the type of structure they need to be successful in their classes. The M-CAPS easily communicates what the student needs to be successful across activities and may be shared with Office of Disabilities staff and college professors. In addition, it supports student self-advocacy. That is, students with ASD can approach faculty members with the M-CAPS and use it as a starting point to discuss student strengths and needs.

In-Class Activities

1. Create an M-CAPS that would help a student with ASD to be successful in this class. (Develop the characteristics of the hypothetical student as needed in order to construct the M-CAPS.)

2. Divide the class into small groups. Assign each of the groups one of the types of activities commonly included on an M-CAPS: (a) independent work, (b) group work, (c) tests, (d) lectures, and (e) homework. Have the groups complete a row of the M-CAPS for the assigned activity for a student in the current class.

Paper Topic Ideas

1. Write a brief essay from the perspective of a parent of a high school student with ASD who has an M-CAPS. What difference does the M-CAPS make for your child? In what way has the M-CAPS improved implementation of your child's IEP? If you were to move to a new school district, what would you tell the new IEP team about the value of the M-CAPS?

2. Write an essay about the M-CAPS from the perspective of a college student who has ASD. How has the M-CAPS improved your ability to self-advocate? What data collection methods are you using? What reinforcers are included on your M-CAPS? Which column on the M-CAPS do you think is most important to your success and why?

Short-Term Project Ideas

1. Create an M-CAPS that would help a student with ASD to be successful in this class. (Develop the characteristics of the hypothetical student as needed in order to construct the M-CAPS.) Include the following activities: (a) independent work, (b) group work, (c) tests, (d) lectures, and (e) homework.

2. Create an M-CAPS that would help you, as a student, to be successful in this class. Include the following activities: (a) independent work, (b) group work, (c) tests, (d) lectures, and (e) homework.

Long-Term Project Ideas

1. Complete an M-CAPS for the student for whom you have created the CAPS during this course. Project to the next level of education (elementary to middle school, middle school to high school, high school to college, college to graduate school) for this student.

The CAPS Process

Learner Objectives

After reading this chapter, the learner should be able to:

- List potential participants on the team that develops the CAPS.

- List and describe the three team member roles.

- Explain the two steps to developing the CAPS.

Chapter Summary

In Chapter Ten, the author discusses how an educational team can facilitate the development of CAPS. Team members assume one of three roles, facilitator, recorder, or team member, all of which are critical to a comprehensive and effective CAPS for the individual student.

Glossary

Baseline CAPS – the status quo for the student; the place at which the team can begin to look at what additional supports are needed

Daily CAPS – includes supports in all areas, as needed, for all activities across the student's day. This CAPS becomes the student's program

Facilitator – usually a current team member with a general understanding of the student; the facilitator explains the process, enlists team members, and ensures that all team members take ownership of the process and follow through with commitments

Recorder – someone on the team with strong clerical skills. The recorder will be key to making sure the team has good documentation of the student's CAPS and that it is disseminated in a timely manner to all involved

Review Questions and Answers

1. Who is the facilitator?

   Answer: This person is usually a current team member with a general understanding of the student. It may be the school psychologist, general educator, special educator, speech-language pathologist, occupational therapist, physical therapist, parent, or anyone with a vested interest in the student's education.

2. What is the role of the facilitator?

   Answer:

   Explains the process

   Enlists team members

   Ensures that all team members take ownership of the process and follow through with commitments

3. Who is the recorder?

   Answer: The recorder may be any one of the team members present. The team should choose someone with strong clerical skills. The recorder will be key to making sure the team has good documentation of the student's CAPS and that it is disseminated in a timely manner to all involved.

4. What is the role of the recorder?

   Answer: The recorder uses the CAPS form to record the supports for the target student. It is recommended that the recording occur on a computer linked to a projection system. This allows all team members to view the process as it occurs, and the completed documents can be distributed immediately to all team members.

5. Who are the team members?

Answer: All other individuals on the multidisciplinary team serve in the role of team members.

6. What is the role of the team members?

Answer: All other team members participate in providing information, as well as contributing any additional strategies and supports per each area outlined in the CAPS framework.

7. What are the two steps of the CAPS process?

Answer:

Step 1: Baseline CAPS. The baseline CAPS represents the status quo for the student – the place at which the team can begin to look at what additional supports are needed. It is important that, when created, this document becomes a part of the student archives, since it allows for easy identification of student growth.

Step 2: Daily CAPS. As detailed in this chapter, the daily CAPS is developed by the team based on the student's need. This CAPS includes supports in all areas, as needed, for all activities across the student's day. This CAPS becomes the student's program.

In-Class Activities

1. Create small groups of three or four. Have each group complete the CAPS process on a case familiar to the whole team. (You may choose to provide a case study.) Rotate roles every 10 minutes until each team member has participated in all three team member roles. Return to the large group and discuss the challenges faced and insights gained.

2. Discuss the value of the baseline CAPS. Discuss the feelings that team members might experience during and after developing the baseline CAPS. What attitudes and principles should guide the creation of the baseline CAPS?

3. Discuss what strategies school administrators, including special education administrators and school principals, could use to maximize the benefits of completing a baseline CAPS and to minimize any perception of risk.

4. Have class members work in pairs. Have the team members exchange CAPS that they have completed. Have each team member take the role of a teacher or other staff member who is to follow through on the CAPS created by the other team member. Have the person in the teacher or other staff member role explain to the CAPS developer the strategies for which he or she would be responsible. Have the CAPS developer make notes and adjustments to the CAPS based on any areas that are not clear.

Return to the large group and discuss the types of clarifications that were helpful. Be certain to reinforce those who share changes that were made. This will help to model acceptance of the review and modifications that result in program improvements.

Paper Topic Ideas

1. Write a brief essay about what strategies school administrators, including special education administrators and school principals, could use to maximize the benefits of completing a baseline CAPS and to minimize any perception of risk.

2. Write a brief essay about the value of the baseline CAPS. Discuss the feelings that team members might experience during and after the developing the baseline CAPS. What attitudes and principles should guide the creation of the baseline CAPS?

Short-Term Project Ideas

1. Working with a team of at least three other people, take the role of the facilitator. Lead the team to develop a CAPS on a student with whom you are each familiar.

2. Share a CAPS with the staff members who are expected to follow through with the strategies. Ask each to tell you what their understanding is of what they will be expected to do for each row on the CAPS. Revise the CAPS for clarity as needed.

Long-Term Project Ideas

1. Compare the CAPS that you have developed and revised as you have completed each chapter to the original version of the same CAPS. Write a brief summary of the improvements that you have made to the original version. Further, discuss the improvements that you have noted in the student's program and progress that you attribute, at least in part, to the CAPS.

References

Aspy, R., & Grossman, B. G. (2011). *The Ziggurat model: A framework for designing comprehensive interventions for individuals with high-functioning autism and Asperger Syndrome – Updated and expanded edition.* Shawnee Mission, KS: AAPC Publishing.

Cooper, J. O., Heron, T. E., & Heward, W. L. (2007). *Applied behavior analysis* (2nd ed.). Upper Saddle River, NJ: Pearson Education.

DeLeon, I., & Iwata, B. A. (1996). Evaluation of a multiple-stimulus presentation format for assessing reinforcer preferences. *Journal of Applied Behavior Analysis, 29,* 519-533.

Didden, R., deMoor, J. M., & Bruyns, W. (1997). Effectiveness of DRO tokens in decreasing disruptive behaviors in the classroom with five multiply handicapped children. *Behavioral Interventions, 12,* 65-75.

Downing, J. A. (2007). *Students with emotional and behavioral problems: Assessment, management and intervention strategies.* Saddle River, NJ: Merrill/Prentice Hall.

Fisher, W. W., Piazza, C. C., Bowman, L. G., & Amari, A. (1996). Integrating caregiver report with a systematic choice assessment to enhance reinforcer identification. *American Journal on Mental Retardation, 101,* 15-25.

Frost, L., & Bondy, A. (2002). *The Picture Exchange Communication System training manual* (2nd ed.). Newark: DE: Pyramid Educational Products.

Printed in the USA
CPSIA information can be obtained
at www.ICGtesting.com
JSHW060850080823
45951JS00001B/1